PRESENT
not perfect
FOR MOMS

◇—◇—◇—◇—◇—◇—◇—◇—◇—◇

A JOURNAL FOR SLOWING DOWN, BEING MINDFUL, AND TRUSTING IN YOURSELF

Aimee Chase

CASTLE POINT BOOKS
NEW YORK

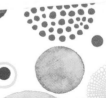
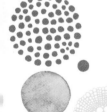

D1372686

♥

THIS JOURNAL BELONGS TO

DON'T ASK YOURSELF AT THE
END OF THE DAY IF YOU DID
EVERYTHING RIGHT. ASK YOURSELF
WHAT YOU LEARNED AND
HOW WELL
YOU LOVED,
THEN GROW FROM
YOUR ANSWER.

—L.R. KNOST

INTRODUCTION

As a mom, you're always trying to do better. Maybe you wish you spent more time with your kids, had more patience with them, cooked healthier meals, or had a cleaner house. Imagine if—from this day on—you could stop trying to be perfect and learn to simply accept and enjoy who you are and all that you have.

Present, Not Perfect for Moms is an invitation to flip your perspective from critical to mindful. Let this journal ease the pressure you put on yourself and highlight the everyday miracles that abound: the feeling of that little hand in yours; the pride of watching them reach a new stage; the peace that comes from knowing they're tucked safely in bed.

Inside you'll find inspiring quotes and thoughtful prompts to awaken gratitude, positivity, and joy whenever you need it. Turn to this artful little book every day to acknowledge all the things you're doing right as a parent and to love your perfectly imperfect life with all you've got.

Right from the Start

Revisit the time when you first realized you wanted to become a mom. Describe that feeling. Was it an instinctual pull, a natural next step, a leap of faith, or a combination?

NOTICE HOW FAR YOU'VE COME TO ARRIVE AT THIS MOMENT. DESCRIBE HOW IT FEELS TO BE A MOM.

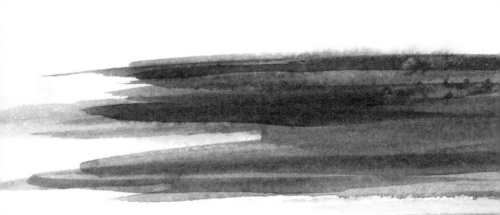

WHAT YOU PLANT NOW, YOU WILL HARVEST LATER.

—OG MANDINO

SEEDS OF LOVE

Take pride in the way your kids look to you as an example. Whether you know it or not, you've taught them so much just by being you. What good habits or ideas are you planting in your children?

WHAT DO YOU HOPE WILL FLOWER IN THEM AS THEY GROW?

YOUR INNER VOICE

Notice the running commentary you have with yourself as you go about your day. Are the messages you give yourself critical or encouraging?

PRACTICE POSITIVE INNER TALK BY PAYING YOURSELF SOME COMPLIMENTS BELOW:

I'm a _____ mom.

I'm incredible at _____.

No one can _____ like I can!

My kid thinks I'm the best

_____.

find more
to love
about
yourself

Freeze Frame

Today, avoid the temptation to rush and practice lingering mindfully in the moment. If you're with your child, take a good look at their face and describe what you see or feel below.

WHAT ARE SOME ACTIVITIES
OR ROUTINES THAT ALLOW YOU TO
CONNECT WITH YOUR KIDS?

HOW CAN YOU ADD MORE OF THESE
ACTIVITIES TO YOUR LIFE?

A JOYFUL HEART
IS THE NORMAL RESULT
OF A HEART
BURNING WITH LOVE.
SHE GIVES MOST
WHO GIVES WITH JOY.

—MOTHER TERESA

FROM MY HEART TO YOURS

WHAT DO YOU LOVE DOING FOR YOUR CHILDREN?
HOW DOES IT MAKE YOU FEEL?

What gifts did your kids offer you this week? Maybe they trusted you enough to ask your advice, hugged you when you least expected it, or offered to help you with something.

It Takes a Village

When parenting has you feeling stretched to your limit, remember to tap into your village. Who are the people in your life that surround you and your child/children with love and support? Write their names on the shapes below.

WHAT HAS YOUR VILLAGE DONE LATELY
THAT MAKES YOU FEEL GRATEFUL?

1.

2.

3.

4.

5.

6.

Notions of Success

Take a moment to evaluate the standards you set for yourself as a parent. In what areas do you give yourself room to fail, to learn, and to begin again?

IN WHAT AREAS DO YOU PUSH YOURSELF TOWARD PERFECTION? SET A MORE REASONABLE EXPECTATION FOR YOURSELF BELOW.

WHAT DO THE ANSWERS ABOVE REVEAL ABOUT YOU?

KINDNESS CONFETTI

Inspire a community of positivity today. Think of a few great moms in your life. Write a sentence of praise to a couple of moms below. Take a snapshot of this page and send it on to brighten their day.

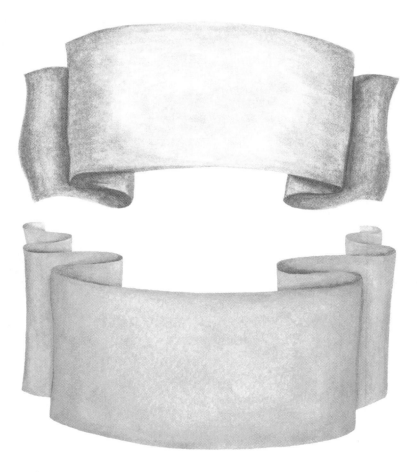

OFFER YOURSELF THE SAME GENEROSITY. WHAT MIGHT THESE MOMS SAY TO YOU?

THE SIGNIFICANCE IS HIDING IN THE INSIGNIFICANT. APPRECIATE EVERYTHING.

—ECKHART TOLLE

THE BIGGEST LITTLE THINGS

What small, everyday moments with your child mean the most to you?

CATCH A BREAK

CARVE OUT AT LEAST ONE FULL MINUTE EVERY DAY FOR A SHORT MINDFULNESS BREAK.

Find a quiet spot where you can sit and close your eyes. Focus on your breathing until you feel centered and calm and more yourself. If it helps, press a hand to your chest and feel your heartbeat. If thoughts come to mind, acknowledge them, let them pass, and return to your breath.

WRITE DOWN ANY THOUGHTS OR FEELINGS YOU HAD WHILE YOU WERE FOCUSED ON YOUR BREATH.

Live in the
HERE AND NOW

TAKE YOUR TASK LIST TO TASK

TAKE A MOMENT TO LIST ALL OF THE EMAILS, ERRANDS,
AND TASKS YOU COMPLETED SO FAR TODAY.

EXHAUSTED YET? DON'T LET YOUR TO-DO LIST FOOL YOU:
This day is not a race. Transform that checklist mentality into a resolve to accomplish less and appreciate more.

SQUELCH THAT NAGGING SENSE OF URGENCY
AND OBSERVE WHAT'S HAPPENING AROUND YOU RIGHT NOW.
USE ALL OF YOUR SENSES TO DESCRIBE IT.

A Stretch of Time

What do you notice right now about your child? Take a mental snapshot of him/her and savor this moment.

WHAT DO YOU NOTICE ABOUT YOURSELF TODAY (BODY, MIND, AND SOUL)?

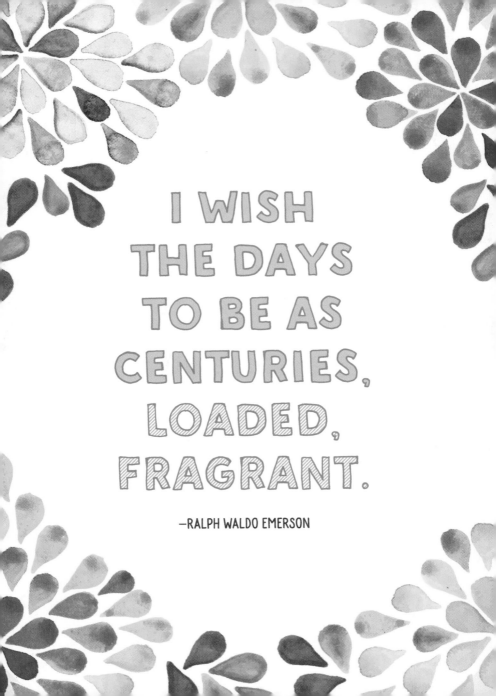

I WISH
THE DAYS
TO BE AS
CENTURIES,
LOADED,
FRAGRANT.

—RALPH WALDO EMERSON

BE
UNAPOLOGETICALLY
YOU

COLOR OUTSIDE THE LINES

Give your imperfections a friendly nod today. What beautiful quirks, funny flaws, or unique traits help to make you an even better mom?

WHAT ARE YOUR CHILD'S MOST UNIQUE TRAITS,
AND HOW CAN YOU TEACH HIM/HER TO VALUE THEM?

THE MOST PRECIOUS GIFT WE CAN OFFER OTHERS IS OUR PRESENCE. WHEN MINDFULNESS EMBRACES THOSE WE LOVE, THEY WILL BLOOM LIKE FLOWERS.

—THÍCH NHẤT HẠNH

WAKING MOMENTS

When have you struggled to be present with your child(ren)?
What got in the way?

DESCRIBE A MINDFUL MOMENT SPENT WITH YOUR CHILD. HOW DID IT FEEL? HOW CAN YOU OPEN YOUR LIFE TO MORE OF THESE MOMENTS?

Trinkets of the Past

Since there's no manual for being a mother, we often look to our own parents for hints. What do you appreciate most about your parents or your upbringing?

WHAT EXPERIENCES FROM YOUR CHILDHOOD WOULD YOU LIKE TO PASS DOWN TO YOUR KIDS?

HOW DO YOU SEE YOUR PARENTS DIFFERENTLY NOW THAT YOU'RE A PARENT?

A LESSON FROM THE LITTLES

Young kids are naturals at living mindfully. They know the wonder of small things, they live in the moment, and they laugh easily.

WHEN HAS YOUR CHILD TAUGHT **YOU** SOMETHING ABOUT MINDFULNESS OR LETTING GO?

Live
and Love
with
Abandon

Sunshine in a Bottle

Every now and then, stop to remind yourself of the little moments you wish you could preserve forever. Those are the moments that matter most. Collect today's sparks of joy here:

SET WIDE
THE WINDOW.
LET ME
DRINK
THE DAY.

—EDITH WHARTON

YOU'VE
GOT THIS

WHAT FILLS YOU WITH PRIDE IN YOURSELF OR YOUR CHILD?

WHAT ARE THE CHALLENGES YOU FACE AS A MOTHER? HOW HAVE YOU SUCCEEDED IN FINDING YOUR WAY THROUGH THEM?

Let the Sun
Shine In

HAPPY JUST HAPPENS

Thinking of happiness as an accomplishment or something you can arrange is bound to leave you feeling like you're grasping at air. Think of happiness, instead, as a state of hopeful surrender to the surprises your day might bring. Describe a recent day that brimmed with unexpected joy.

HOW CAN YOU LET
HAPPINESS FIND YOU?

MINDFUL IN A MINUTE

Being busy doesn't mean you can't be mindful. Even everyday tasks are an opportunity to notice what you hear, smell, see, touch, and taste in the moment. Circle the tasks you can use to feel more present.

MAKING COFFEE

BRUSHING YOUR TEETH

SHOWERING

FOLDING CLOTHES

**TUCKING YOUR CHILD
INTO BED**

DESCRIBE YOUR EXPERIENCE OF TURNING
A DAILY RITUAL INTO A MINDFUL MOMENT.

WHAT DID YOUR SENSES HELP YOU
NOTICE ABOUT THIS TASK THAT
YOU HADN'T NOTICED BEFORE?

Loosen Your Grip

What are you holding onto a little too tightly these days? Maybe it's the idea that your growing child needs you more than they do; maybe you're trying to maintain an image of perfection for others; or maybe you think you can trick your kids into liking vegetables. Write your answer below.

WHATEVER IT IS, WHAT WOULD
HAPPEN IF YOU LET IT GO?

BLESS THIS MESS

Life is chaotic and complicated and altogether beautiful if done right. If your home is a disorganized array of socks, toys, school papers, and sports equipment, then you're more than likely fully immersed in and devoted to the glorious business of raising children.

WRITE DOWN ALL OF THE MEANINGFUL WAYS YOU USED YOUR TIME TODAY INSTEAD OF AIMING FOR HOUSEHOLD PERFECTION.

MAKE
PEACE
WITH
CHAOS

BE CONSCIOUS OF ANY WEIGHT THAT'S ON YOUR SHOULDERS TODAY.
DESCRIBE IT OR DRAW WHAT IT FEELS LIKE HERE.

WHAT PRESSURES EXIST IN YOUR LIFE?
LIST THEM IN THE CATEGORIES BELOW:

Pressures I Put on Myself   Pressures from Others

Give yourself permission to share your feelings or your
responsibilities with others and lighten your emotional load.

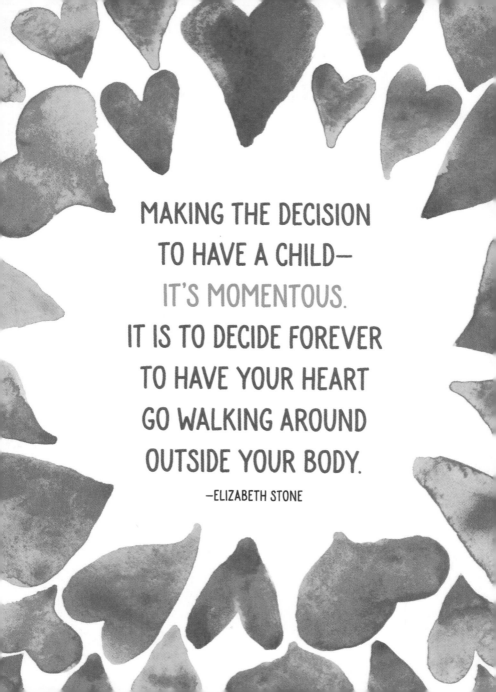

MAKING THE DECISION
TO HAVE A CHILD—
IT'S MOMENTOUS.
IT IS TO DECIDE FOREVER
TO HAVE YOUR HEART
GO WALKING AROUND
OUTSIDE YOUR BODY.

—ELIZABETH STONE

WHEN HAVE YOU FELT LIKE YOUR HEART WAS WALKING AROUND OUTSIDE YOUR BODY?

HOW DO YOU COPE WITH OR MANAGE THE FEELING OF VULNERABILITY THAT COMES WITH LOVE AND PARENTHOOD?

HOW HAVE YOU MODELED MINDFULNESS,
THE IMPORTANCE OF WELL-BEING, OR THE POWER
OF POSITIVITY FOR YOUR KIDS?

WHAT IS THE ART OF LIVING,
IN YOUR OPINION?

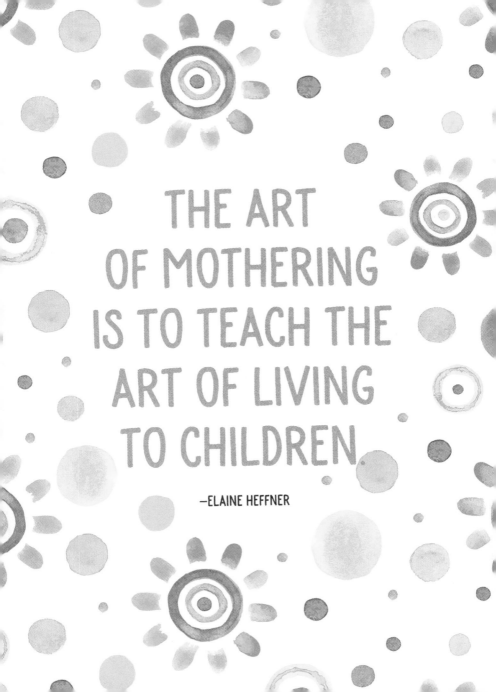

THE ART
OF MOTHERING
IS TO TEACH THE
ART OF LIVING
TO CHILDREN

—ELAINE HEFFNER

Living Your Truth

What about yourself do you tend to hide from others? How can you let it shine?

WHAT'S ONE MISTAKE (BIG OR SMALL) YOU'VE MADE AS A PARENT? HOW DID YOU GROW FROM IT?

Making
Mistakes is
Better Than
Faking
Perfection

The butterfly counts not months but moments,
AND HAS TIME ENOUGH.

—RABINDRANATH TAGORE

THE WORLD WITHIN

Take a mindful moment and lighten your thoughts as you color this pattern and reflect. Imagine other creative ways you could enjoy "pausing" the day.

SCRAPBOOK MOMENTS

Stop to take a meaningful detour from your routine today and spend some mindful moments enjoying your child at this point in time. Record below what you noticed about your child at this stage and how it felt to spend time together.

ADD A PHOTO OF YOUR CHILD (OR CHILDREN)
BELOW THAT SHOWCASES WHAT
YOU LOVE MOST ABOUT THIS AGE.

Use Your Village

To be a good mom, you don't have to be all things to your kids:
you just have to be you. List all the qualities you offer.

POSITIVE

CUDDLY

GOOD LISTENER

ADVOCATE

SPIRITUAL

HOW DO OTHER MEMBERS OF YOUR "VILLAGE"
FILL IN THE MISSING PIECES?

Reject the pressure to win in every parenting category, honor
your strengths, and remind yourself what an incredible mom
you are.

Soul Stirring

WHAT ALWAYS AMAZES YOU ABOUT MOTHERHOOD?

FIND OR WRITE A POEM THAT CAPTURES WHAT
MOTHERHOOD MEANS TO YOU AND ADD IT HERE.

THE TIES THAT BIND

The common threads that connect you and your child strengthen the fabric of your relationship. What physical or emotional qualities do you share with your child?

WHEN DO YOU FEEL MOST
CONNECTED TO YOUR CHILD?

Some bonds
are too deep
for others
to ever
understand.

—SOMAN CHAINANI

More than a Mom

When the house is quiet and the kids are fast asleep, what do you enjoy doing?

WHAT ACTIVITIES OR HOBBIES MAKE YOU FEEL WHOLE?

FIND YOURSELF AGAIN AND AGAIN

STRIVE FOR AUTHENTICITY

Look beyond the perfection of Pinterest, the filters of Instagram, and the glossy sheen of others' expertly marketed lives and strive for a more authentic and fulfilling experience of your own. Treasure the messiest but truest aspects of your life and "post" them here as a reminder of what matters.

THE REASON WE STRUGGLE WITH INSECURITY IS BECAUSE WE COMPARE OUR BEHIND-THE-SCENES WITH EVERYONE ELSE'S HIGHLIGHT REEL.

—STEVE FURTICK

BE THANKFUL
FOR THIS MOMENT.
THIS MOMENT
IS YOUR LIFE.

—OMAR KHAYYAM

MAKE IT COUNT

What part of raising children do you wish would last forever?

WHAT FEELINGS DOES THIS ASPECT OF PARENTING INSPIRE?
HOW CAN YOU ADD MORE OF THESE FEELINGS TO YOUR LIFE?

Foraging for Beauty

Nature doesn't aim to impress; it simply exists. Spend a few minutes outdoors today, with your child or on your own, and observe the authentically imperfect wonders that decorate your life. Look for the items below or record your own list.

A WORN PATH

A CRAGGY ROCK

A BENT BRANCH

A SLOW-WANDERING INSECT

A BIRD'S SONG

Nature is painting for us,
DAY AFTER DAY,
pictures of
infinite beauty.

—JOHN RUSKIN

PASS IT ON

Consider the well of wisdom and strength within you. Share this precious resource with others today. Write a note to a new or expecting mom and impart what you know to be true about motherhood and happiness.

WHAT I LOVE ABOUT YOU

There's no one quite like your baby. Whether your baby is still a baby or has grown by leaps and bounds, unleash your pride as you finish the statements below.

MY KID IS INCREDIBLE BECAUSE . . .

WHAT I LOVE MOST ABOUT MY CHILD IS . . .

THEY'RE BECOMING BETTER AND BETTER AT . . .

WHEN I PICTURE THEM IN THE FUTURE, I SEE . . .

WHEN YOU REALIZE
NOTHING IS LACKING,
**THE WHOLE WORLD
BELONGS TO YOU.**

—LAO TZU

Perfect
is
Boring

The Real Deal

Describe the quirky traits that make each person in your family even more endearing.

LIST ALL THE PEOPLE WHO KNOW AND LOVE
YOU FOR THE PERSON YOU TRULY ARE:

THE TIME
TO RELAX IS
WHEN YOU DON'T
HAVE TIME
FOR IT.

TURN MAYHEM INTO MUSIC

Open your ears to the sounds of your present environment. Sit in stillness until every piece of you is listening. Record your observations below.

DEEP BREATHS
ARE LIKE
LITTLE LOVE NOTES
TO YOUR BODY.

BREATH CONTROL

Stopping to take a few deep breaths is a powerful way to restore balance to your day.

IMAGINE THAT AS YOU INHALE, YOU'RE DRAWING GOLDEN LIGHT, HOPE, AND POSITIVITY INTO YOUR BODY.

WHEN YOU EXHALE, PICTURE DARKNESS, WORRIES, AND NEGATIVITY BEING CAST OUT OF YOUR BODY.

REPEAT UNTIL YOU FEEL MORE CENTERED AND RELAXED. WHAT IMAGES HELP YOU BREATHE MORE EASILY?

Face Your Fears

The best way to conquer feelings of anxiety is to remind yourself that you can handle anything. What are the nagging worries, guilty sentiments, or unsettling fears that keep you from feeling free?

HOW MIGHT THESE CONCERNS BE A MISUSE
OF YOUR TIME AND ENERGY?

WHAT WOULD HAPPEN IF YOU STOPPED WORRYING ALTOGETHER
AND CEASED TO FEEL ANYTHING BUT ALIVE IN THIS MOMENT?

WORRY LESS;
Live More

NOW AND FOREVER

What part of today felt most meaningful?

WHAT FUTURE HOPES AND DREAMS
ADD SUNSHINE TO THE PRESENT?

MOTHERHOOD IS AN ACT OF INFINITE OPTIMISM.

—GILDA RADNER

A ROOM OF ONE'S OWN

Claim an area of your home as your own mindful space. Seek it out when your energy wanes or you lose your sense of balance and you need to retreat for a few moments of serenity. Where is this spot in your home, and how can you add to its peaceful vibe?

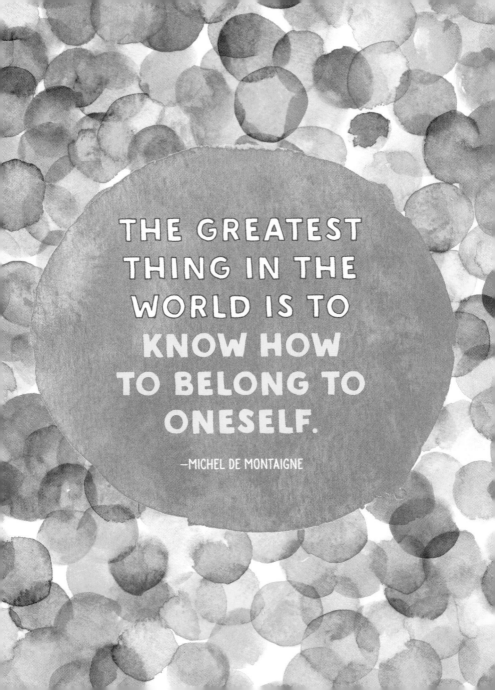

THE GREATEST
THING IN THE
WORLD IS TO
KNOW HOW
TO BELONG TO
ONESELF.

—MICHEL DE MONTAIGNE

Thanks a Bunch

Take a moment to count your blessings. What are you most grateful for today?

WHAT ARE YOU GLAD YOU CAN PROVIDE FOR YOUR CHILDREN?

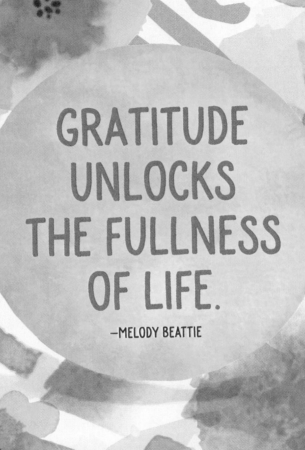

GRATITUDE
UNLOCKS
THE FULLNESS
OF LIFE.

—MELODY BEATTIE

PARENTING ON THE FLY

Instincts and guesswork are the tools we count on as moms. No perfect answers exist when it comes to raising kids. When have you felt like you were winging it as a parent?

WHEN HAVE YOUR INSTINCTS STEERED YOU WELL?

WHAT PARENTING DECISIONS ARE YOU PROUD TO HAVE MADE?

Trust
in
Yourself

WANDER WITHIN

Set a timer for two minutes. Close your eyes and slowly retreat from the noise of the external world to the peace of your inner world. Notice the ebb and flow of your thoughts. Let your feelings breeze through you.

DESCRIBE WHAT WORKED BEST TO CALM YOU IN THE SPACE BELOW.

WHO LOOKS OUTSIDE, DREAMS; *who looks inside, awakens.*

—CARL JUNG

You Need You

Moms are experts in nurturing others, but they can easily forget to honor their own needs in the process. Consider how well you balance taking care of yourself and taking care of your family.

THINGS I'VE DONE FOR MYSELF THIS WEEK	THINGS I'VE DONE FOR OTHERS THIS WEEK

WHAT DO YOU NOTICE ABOUT THE LISTS ABOVE?

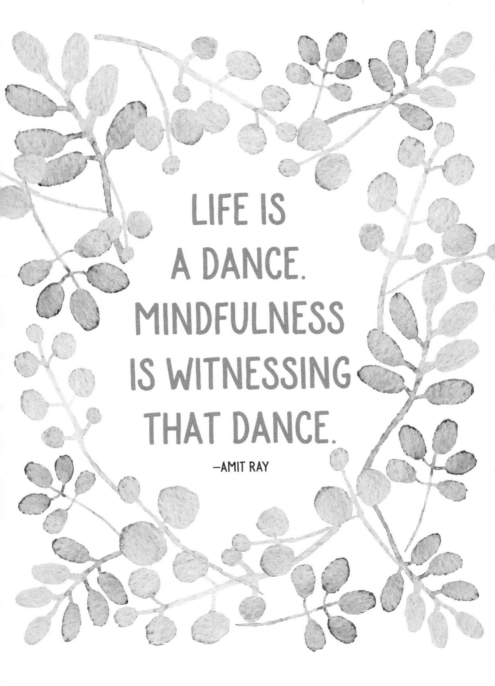

LIFE IS
A DANCE.
MINDFULNESS
IS WITNESSING
THAT DANCE.

—AMIT RAY

POETRY IS EVERYWHERE

Seek out inspiration to add extra sparks of love and light to your job as a parent. Copy the words of a spirit-rousing quote, pay tribute to someone you admire, jot down a moving song lyric, or find a photo of something that speaks to you and add it below.

FEED YOUR SOUL

IN THIS TOGETHER

Describe your partner in parenting. How do they support your role as a mom?

HOW WOULD YOUR SPOUSE OR PARTNER
DESCRIBE YOU AS A MOM?

FILL OUT THE DIAGRAM BELOW TO APPRECIATE THE WAYS
IN WHICH YOUR PARENTING VALUES OVERLAP WITH
AND COMPLEMENT YOUR PARTNER'S VALUES.

**MATTERS MOST
TO ME**

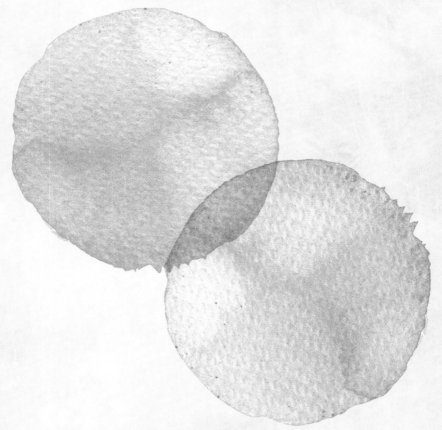

**MATTERS MOST
TO MY PARTNER**

Open Every Door

List three people or circumstances that help you be the mom you've always wanted to be. Take a moment to appreciate these gifts in your life.

1.

2.

3.

Name three changes that would make your job as a mom even easier.

1.

2.

3.

What doors could you open to add these elements to your life?

ASK FOR
WHAT YOU NEED

DEEP DIVING

You are more than the parade of thoughts marching through your brain. Find the "you" beneath the surface today. Unfurl the busy contents of your mind below and see if it brings you a greater sense of peace.

Quiet the mind,

AND THE SOUL WILL SPEAK.

—MA JAYA SATI BHAGAVATI

PEACE IN PROGRESS

When has mindfulness, that loving embrace of the present moment, been helpful to you?

WHAT TECHNIQUES OR STRATEGIES HELP YOU FIND CALM AND PEACE ON STRESSFUL DAYS?

Breathe in HAPPINESS; Breathe out STRESS

Sowing Your Love

Consider the depth of your love for your child. Write down all the wishes you have for them and their future.

Imagine that you are blowing gently on the dandelions below, releasing wonderous possibilities and seeds of promise along their path.

STRONG ENOUGH FOR BOTH OF US

What strengths has parenting allowed you to discover in yourself? Write them proudly on the mountain ranges below.

YOUR LOVE
CAN MOVE
MOUNTAINS

NOTHING TO HIDE

WHAT INSECURITIES DO YOU KEEP HIDDEN FROM THE WORLD?

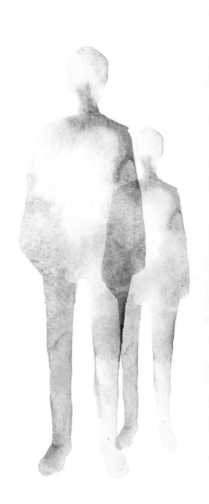

WHAT DO YOU NEED TO REMIND YOURSELF OF IN ORDER TO CONQUER THESE INSECURITIES? WRITE AN ENCOURAGING MESSAGE TO YOURSELF BELOW.

HOW MIGHT OVERCOMING THESE INSECURITIES MAKE YOU A BETTER MOM?

Release Your Expectations

Write a note to yourself below where you give yourself permission to be imperfect.

AIM FOR
GROWTH;
NOT
PERFECTION

LIVING IN THE NOW

Find a way to sprinkle some mindfulness into your day. Whether it's putting your to-do list aside, noticing when your inner critic arises, or putting your cell phone down and looking deep into your child's eyes, being present in the moment makes life more joyful. Plan how to add a few mindful moments to your day below.

IN THE MIDST OF CHAOS, THERE IS ALSO OPPORTUNITY.

—SUN TZU

ALL KNOW
THE WAY,
BUT FEW
ACTUALLY
WALK IT.

—BODHIDHARMA

HOW FAR YOU'VE COME

What have you learned so far from walking the path of parenting? Write those lessons on the bricks below.

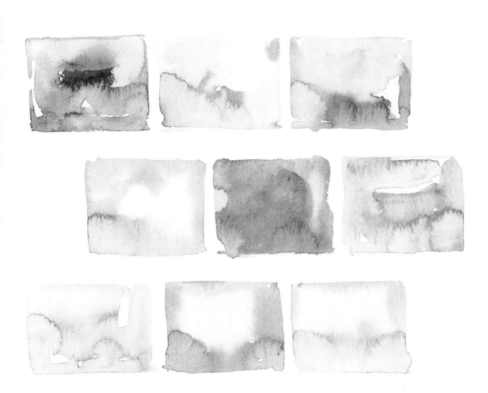

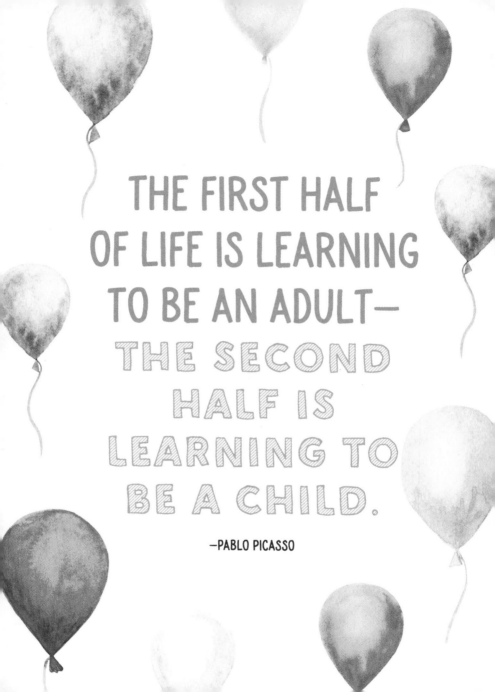

THE FIRST HALF
OF LIFE IS LEARNING
TO BE AN ADULT—
THE SECOND
HALF IS
LEARNING TO
BE A CHILD.

—PABLO PICASSO

BEING A MOM DOESN'T MEAN YOU HAVE TO BE ALL BUSINESS ALL THE TIME.

Strive for a healthy balance of work and play. Invite laughter and lightness into your day whenever you feel tension rising. What thrills you, makes you feel alive, or causes you to burst into laughter?

A Light in the Harbor

At the end of the day, you're a safe haven for your child. You're a lighthouse in the storm. List all the wonderful ways in which they can count on you for support and guidance.

MOMENTS THAT MATTER

What did you enjoy most about your child as a baby? Describe a moment that stands out in your mind.

WHAT ASPECT OF PARENTING ARE YOU EMBRACING
WHOLE-HEARTEDLY RIGHT NOW?

WHAT WILL YOU ALWAYS REMEMBER ABOUT THIS TIME?

Life isn't a matter of milestones, but of moments.

—ROSE KENNEDY

ADD AN IMAGE OF YOU AND YOUR FAMILY HERE.

COME BACK TO THIS IMAGE WHENEVER YOU NEED
A REMINDER THAT **YOU ARE ENOUGH**.

YOU HAVE CREATED **A WHOLE WORLD OF LOVE**
FOR YOUR CHILD, AND THAT, OF COURSE, IS *EVERYTHING*.